the
Barbie
diaries

to Carolyn

Dale Champlin
with gratitude

Cover Photograph, Design and Layout
Dale Champlin

Author Photograph
Lisa Champlin Story

Back Cover
X-ray photograph of frogs, c.1896
An x-ray photograph of frogs created by Josef Maria Eder
and Eduard Valentia, taken from *Versuche über Photographie
mittelst der Röntgen Strahlen* (Vienna, 1896)

Published by
Just a Lark Books
308 SE Walnut Street

JUST A LARK BOOKS
Hillsboro, Oregon

Body copy set in Caslon 540

First edition

10 9 8 7 6 5 4 3 2 1

ISBN 9781708450267

Who knew you could write an epic poem about Barbie?
Dale Champlin has done it. *The Barbie Diaries* opens with fresh
insights into the usual Barbie-Ken tropes and then moves,
always at Barbie-scale, into the larger vicissitudes of time.
This collection is completely charming. You will laugh at the
early poems. The later poems may bring you
to the edge of weeping.

—Penelope Scambly Schott
feminist poet
Winner of the Oregon Book Award in poetry for
A Is for Anne: Mistress Hutchinson Disturbs the Commonwealth

Foreword

This funny, sexy and sometimes harrowing collection of poems is a refreshing look at ourselves through the unexpectedly human eyes of Barbie.

Not only is she an icon of feminine perfection but an observer who misses nothing and deeply feels the joys, losses and longings of life.

Barbie's devotion to her girl, the freedom of cutting loose with Ken and the secret pleasures of new relationships are contrasted with the cuts of misogyny, the cruelties of adolescence and the desolation of abandonment.

A stroke of bad luck lands Barbie in an extended confinement and gives her time to muse and reflect on the changing seasons, the briefness of childhood and the price of immortality. Barbie is a survivor.

Dale Champlin has given Barbie such a strong voice and persona in this smart and engrossing collection that it's hard to realize these poems have not been found in some secret trove of Barbie's personal papers.

for my husband,
who is nothing like Ken

Contents

THE YEAR BARBIE SPENT AT THE BOTTOM OF THE POOL

HOME AT LAST

Writing Weird

Since you left I've been writing weird.
In my effort not to crawl back to you,
I starved myself to a whisker moon.
Alone in lostness, with my new Barbie body,
I teeter across the four-lane in six-inch stilettos,
without a blink of my swimming-pool-blue eyes.
All four lanes screech to a stop. It must be
that my waist-length bleached-blond tresses
blind those attention-starved drivers.

I remember our camping trip to Reno
in my bubblegum-pink convertible camper
with its cabana awning and fold-up recliners.
We called Route 66 a river, squatted in the motel
and swilled dry martinis. We didn't care
if the beer nuts were stale. We'd cashed in our chips,
sold our condo in Malibu and put the twins
in foster care. Where are you Ken?

I miss your square jaw.

Barbie's Sex Life

Is up for grabs. Ken has his secrets. And what's with that hunky Australian surfer guy who's always hanging around? These ridiculous stilettos are killing her feet all the way up her back. Barbie can't stand flat on the floor even if she wants to. Plus she's starved for attention, not the "Let's cut off all her hair," kind but more like, "Where's her vagina anyway?" She's been working on her abs and her kegles. One – two, she clenches her buttocks together. Barbie suspects that Ken is working on his kegels too. Barbie looks at her chest, sure her breasts will never sag. Right now she's naked under the bed, not on top of it, one leg twisted over her head. She would cry if she could.

But what if Ken doesn't have a penis?

Possession

I was her first Barbie.
She used to carry me everywhere—
prop me by her bowl
and feed me chocolate ice cream.
She held me in her arms
and took me to bed at night—
then she lost one of my shoes,
my leg joint got loose.
She tattooed her name on my back
with a ball-point pen
and nail polished
my nipples day-glo.
After her mom's hairdryer
scorched my hair
she cut off the burnt ends.
It was not an improvement.
I thought I was priceless,
but I was replaceable.
I can't leave it up to Ken
to rescue me. He's preoccupied
with his wardrobe.
His stone-cold eyes
never glance in my direction.
Once he told me to get a job,
but with my tiny hands
I can't hold more than a sliver.

Terrible Fun

And the stars may never again shine as now they shine

—Emily Brontê

Hey Ken, remember that first night
of malt liquor and tequila shots
in a bar near Motel 6?
I was so blotto I only wanted sex—
plain and white as an oyster cracker.
When we staggered out of the dive
stars clustered in patterns above the parking lot.
You made out a crematorium smokestack—
I spotted a Ferris wheel, a squirrel
and a walking Chatty Cathy doll.
We sloshed into your dented Toyota Corolla.
I should have guessed by your plastic pompadour
that you'd be into S&M. You let me pee
in your bathroom, toiletries spread
all over the grime. The place reeked
of Old Spice aftershave and dried piss.
Your turn in the John you griped
about my "unmentionables," as if!
I lay naked on the grubby bedspread.
You loomed above me scrawny as a coyote—
wicked buzzard rough—
sharp pelvis primed for grinding—
looped a twistem around my wrists
and told me to roll over. Quick as anything,
you slid a bit between my teeth, martingales
on either side kept me from lifting my head.
You rode me like a demon—
clenched me in a choke hold, snakebit my neck,
and hard knuckled my thighs. I was afraid
you would put me up for sale on eBay.
I was so tight I couldn't even queef.
After you flipped me over,
you told me my tits
looked like dead rabbits.

If I Only Had a Brain

Barbie has started to write poetry.
For her, time seems to stand still.
She believes in life on distant planets.
The people might look like her.
She can see plenty outside her window.
She imagines the universe is much larger
than the house she lives in. She imagines
dinosaurs roaming about in her back yard.
The thought of black holes terrifies her.
She doesn't believe in ghosts, witches or vampires.
She is more concerned with dust bunnies
and the half-life of plastic.
Barbie believes in surrealism, rain, and bitcoins.
Before writing a poem, Barbie thinks for an hour.
Since time is illusory, she may be thinking
longer than she realizes.
Fashion is what she thinks about mostly—
stilettos, tulle, polyester and pencil skirts.
It would be wonderful to get an MFA in poetry
but where could she teach?
Most people don't take her seriously.
Last week someone told her her eyes
are blue as a Caribbean lagoon.
That would be a great first line in a poem.
Barbie is a millennial. Once, she read a funny poem
about empathic animals and a tragic one
about a toy ballerina and a lead soldier.
She decides to write an imagist poem.
Small buds unfurling into tiny hands press my window.
The poem isn't working yet but that's life.
Ken doesn't talk to her about her poem.
Maybe he can't read.

Being Married to Ken

is not a joy ride,
or a rollercoaster ride
it is slower and rougher—
like hiking through scree
at the foot of a mountain
or stumbling over crumbling
logs—tripping once or twice
to land on one knee
in rotting leaf mold—
or trying to sleep in a pup tent
when it's freezing outside
and moisture condenses
on the inside walls of the tent
and drips into your hair—
mosquitos whine
and there are probably
spiders, mice and even a snake.
But so far our marriage has survived
and thankfully the mastodons
are long gone.

That Night

There is nothing to be afraid of,
he told the little girl,
I'm your brother after all,
your reflection in the mirror,
your bookend. Come and sit
on my quilt and I will tell you
a bedtime story. Listen
to the rain on the roof,
how the wind thrashes
the leaves. My hands
will keep you warm.
Put your face near mine
so I can smell your breath.
Put your feet between my thighs
and don't call for mother.
She doesn't want to hear you snivel.
Come under the covers and lift up
your nightie just so. I will rock
you to the patter of acorns
hitting the roof. Don't worry—
it's just an owl hooting
in the tree outside the window.
That screeching you hear
is only a branch
needling the windowpane.

Like an Angel

When I saw myself reflected
in the mirror—
cold-shouldered, stiff
as a garden rake
drifting in chiffon
like frozen motion,
almost weightless,
decked in sparkle-feathers,
I thought I must be an angel
and yet—
I saw myself as if stunned
into silence—
a petal-mouthed child-woman
inflexible and obstinate.
My face would never twist
in disappointment,
my voice would never howl
in pleasure or pain,
my neon-blue eyes
would never tear.

Barbie's Pleasure Cruise

When Ken and I took a cruise
to the Bahamas he made sure
I was aware that we were drinking
used water. By the end of the trip
every sip would have passed
through hundreds of bladders.

Our immense ship—one of the Queens,
made for extended intimacy—our
overused cabin, my mildewed bikinis,
Ken sulking whenever he lost at shuffleboard.
Adrift beyond my control, my mood
steely blue as the ocean at dusk.

After each meal deckhands threw
leftovers overboard where they attracted
sharks and screaming seagulls. When
they locked up the jock who shoved
his fiancé into the wake of the ship,
I understood why he'd pushed her.

Back then the Atlantic was already
a wasteland—whaleless, deserted.
Even so I kept searching for a plume
or a lighthouse on the horizon.
Each night the moon shone like a flashlight
over the wrinkled skin of the sea.

I prayed for an iceberg
to break up the monotony.

Barbie is Just Like all the Girls

I always knew Ken loved me.
The way his hands fit
around my ridiculously small waist
and his eyes peered into mine.

I believed
I was the only one for him.
Sometimes, I dreamed he entered me from above
after he rose from his shoebox coffin.
Sometimes he held me hard.
One entire summer he was lost
behind the doghouse.
My little girl found him in the fall,
scorched golden—godlike.

I wondered
if he would ever come back to me.
He came less and less. He said
it was because of the crow's feet
around my eyes. His shrunken hands
no longer fit around my waist.
He was impatient and wondered why
I never gave him a baby Ken
after all our years of trying.

I questioned
if I would ever see him again.
Could he find me in the bottom drawer
or pressed folded double into a high-top,
stripped of my hair and makeup,
my clothes tossed into the rag bin.

The last time I saw him he turned his eyes
away. He pretended he didn't know me.
But I saw him standing there—
his Elvis suit as tight on his hips
as a condom.

Ken Has His Say

I always wished the best for Barbie.
She used to be so beautiful.
I would gaze at her in her
plastic display box
and wonder what she was thinking.
I thought she might be anorexic
because of her ridiculously small waist
but I knew it was impossible—
her shoulders and breasts were so full
and her tresses so luxurious.

After she got out of her wrapper
her hair started to snarl and tangle.
She lost her underwear.
She was still beautiful
in a feral way, until
one of the neighbor kids
got hold of her,
burned all her clothes,
and threw her under the porch
where the cat peed on her.

The girl found her
and washed her with shampoo.
The cat smell is less
but not entirely gone.
I could still love her—
a little. But things are different now.
I have a job at the bank
and a new Ferrari. After all,
I have my image to consider.

Plain Old Barbie

What is it about my life
that I find beauty in how
moss coats rocks?
—Barbie

Before she went to college
my girl taught me to smooth the wrinkles
from tin foil with a wooden spoon.
I perfected hospital corners when we made her bed.
I didn't go to school with her. I never read a book.

But I remember her kind brown eyes
and the way one of her eyebrows
was interrupted by a mole.
Now I sip coffee and whiskey neat.
God only knows how I learned to drive.

I love to careen my bubblegum-pink Corvette
eighty on twisty mountain roads.
I don't go to church on Sunday
or write poetry. I watch birds fly in formation
but I've never seen snow.
I don't like to think too hard.
Like Cyndi Lauper, I just want to have fun!

Barbie Can't Swim

I don't like pools.
I was never good at swimming.
I overthink the process—
all that soupy chlorine,
the drain at the bottom
constantly sucking,
how my hair might get tangled
or the sun could bleach the plastic
on one side of my torso.
How my neck won't bend properly
to keep my head above water
and how it's impossible for me
to shut my eyes.

I don't trust love.
It feels too much like drowning.
If I had a heart it might break
or melt. I know my little girl loves me—
for now. Once when her brother
threw me into the pool,
I felt my joints leak,
the water could only float me
for so long. She jumped right in
without a thought for herself.
She could have died.

She would have been sad
to lose me. She must know
there are other Barbies.
I didn't think I could love
anyone as much as Ken.
But when my little girl sacrificed
her safety for me, I realized
Ken's love was only
surface deep.

Who Lifted Barbie Up?

I wonder what it would be like
to float on top of the sea.
Would I be a mermaid
cradled in foam?

Would my little girl rescue me
and sing me to sleep in her dinghy,
rocking gently up and down
under a ladder of starlight?

Divorce

When Ken came back from
Australia, tanned, and talking
with that weird accent, I knew
I couldn't take anymore.

I didn't want him anywhere near
my McMansion with its infinity
pool and skylights on the shed roof,
especially since he totaled my Maserati
the day before he left.

I could let him sleep on the sectional
but I would be able to hear him snoring
all the way upstairs.

Sometimes at night I see him
out on the deck, his topsiders
side-by-side under one of the chaises.

He would make a pretty cute pool boy
but what would the neighbors think?

Playing Doctor

My little girl's brother is sharpening his tools—
toothpicks, nail clippers, pocketknife.
He gets home from school early to raid
my shoebox, takes me over to his desk
and turns on his lamp.

I lie naked on his operating table.
This is his idea of "playing doctor."
First he amputates one leg, then the other.
I don't bleed. I think of pink balloons
and unicorns.

I need to remain calm. All the while
a voice inside my head is screaming—
Not my head, not my head!
After he rips my head off he turns up
the sound on his headphones.

He tapes my head back on
and runs a Popsicle stick up my back
for a splint. He wraps me with
Kleenex from head to toe
and daubs it with red nail polish.

In My Shoebox

Beside me, a chopped-off
braid of my little girl's hair
in a twist of faded pink ribbon
her white silk diary unlocked
the key lost many years ago.
A note she copied from Emily
I have been very ill,
bereft of Book and Thought.
but I begin to roam in my room,
scrawled in her childish cursive.
Now I write in her diary,
a mechanical pencil-lead
clenched between my
outstretched thumb and fingers.
I lie in the dark
in a tattered shoebox
tucked beneath the bed.

Poseable Doll

He wants her arranged just so.
He wants her, arranged.
He arranges to want her.

—Margaret Atwood, "Iconography"

Under my own devices
my left arm hangs straight
from my shoulder. The other
crimps at a right angle.
My feet maintain a painful demi-point—
bound Chinese lotus blossoms.

I am no Ballerina Barbie—
flexible, graceful, delicate—
a ballerina in her pretty pink tutu.
My waist can't swivel
and my legs don't bend,
but I can rotate my head like an owl
and raise each leg in a high-kick.

Her brother wants to arrange me.
Over and over he poses me to his whim.
After he thrusts my hips into position—
my submissive tango begins. He tips
my torso back and clutches my buttocks.
I swoop and swoon. If I turn my head
and try to resist, he forces me back to attention.

Then out comes the silver thread
compelling as spider silk. He stretches
my arms over my head, splays
my legs apart. Sculpted, I hang
from a guywire. Am I his puppet
when he makes me over from scratch?

Taxonomy of Lost Things

I am his Bonnie and he is my Clyde/no, I mean, I am his Barbie and he is my Ken/in my neoprene monster skin/in my faux city/ in my broke-down doll house, in my tiny bed/that sleeps my torso, in my souvenir/sombrero, in umbrella shade/or in my die-cast/Corvette, cherry red, sun bright, comet/fast, in that shrunken hour/I cannot hold on to/that shadow-dwindled noontime.

After my little girl's brother kicked me into the gutter/I began to die/I thought I was asleep/dreaming my afterlife, the same as now/like a frog cloaked in pond scum/more flexible/less brittle, toxic plastic/ a scourge to ecology. I missed my cavalcade escapade/neon blue swimming pool/powder pink vestibule/Cadillac Escalade. My little girl found me/Ken had flown to Hong Kong.

After Ken's makeover it wasn't the same/we tried to rekindled our relationship/ our shipwreck of love. Each morning now/I go downstairs; make breakfast wound up like a light bulb/buzzing on the blink, I feel like that frog/fresh from the gutter/we don't sleep in the same bed/I wake up early, everything hurts/my plastic is tattered/my joints black with mold/a rhinestone glued to my cheek.

Sometimes Being Lost is Better than Being Found

Hooligans. The neighborhood wolf pack
invades our split-level. Doors slam,
boys circle the living room,
trash the kitchen, skid down the halls.
They hanker for disruption and havoc—
crowded small spaces and loud rock.

Pseudo-ninjas punch each other in the chest.
When they come-to they are zombified.
Feral boys body-slam, tip over furniture,
spill Coke on our avocado shag carpet.
Figurines shatter, picture frames smash,
toilets clog, cutlery is thrown.

Mother heads for her bedroom—
a bottle of Jim Beam tucked under her arm.
Danger from every direction. It's darn lucky
my little girl isn't here. Her brother
sets my teeth on edge. I cower in my drawer.
He scoops me up. Kidnapped again!
The kid needs an audience—says he's a magician—
fixates on the space between one leg and another.
His thoughts are obsessive.

My memories stir. Right now he's thinking
of the ultimate trick. He has me in a choke hold.
I scream. What does my voice sound like?
I don't know—it's inside my head.
"Hold perfectly still," he says. I see the way
his eyes gleam, small and red as a bat's.
After he saws me in half he throws me into
the recycling bin.

I Don't Want to Think About Love Anymore

—after Patrick Dundon, *After He Said The End*

I'm lost without
my boom box
and sometimes
I even miss Ken
the curve of his thigh
the sneer of his lip
I want to forgive him
for all his indiscretions
I want to lick his face
like a plate
I want to start
all over again
and hear him say
he really really
likes me not just
for my breasts
or my hair or my
long long legs
but when
it comes right
down to it I can't
change for him
and I don't want
to change for

myself and I think
of the last time
we sat at
the kitchen table
laughing and I
cracked a joke
he snorted so
hard milk came
out his nose
then I think of
palm fronds
and dinosaur flesh
roiling under the
bones of the earth
syphoned
as petroleum
and concocted
into the ethylene-
vinyl acetate
that he and I
are both made of
our clarity and gloss
only skin deep
but that's not love.

I Don't Want to Think About Love Anymore

I'm lost without
my boom box
and sometimes
I even miss Ken
the curve of his thigh
the sneer of his lip
I want to forgive him
for all his indiscretions
I want to lick his face
like a plate
I want to start
all over again
and hear him say
he really really
likes me not just
for my breasts
or my hair or my
long long legs
but when
it comes right
down to it I can't
change for him
and I don't want
to change for
myself and I think
of the last time
we sat at
the kitchen table
laughing and I
cracked a joke

he snorted so
hard milk came
out his nose
then I think of
palm fronds
and dinosaur flesh
roiling under the
bones of the earth
syphoned
as petroleum
and concocted
into the ethylene-
vinyl acetate
that he and I
are both made of
our clarity and gloss
only skin deep
but that's not love.

The Year
Barbie Spent
at the Bottom
of the Pool

Day 1

Barbie's not surprised.
The last day of summer—
what a shark fest! Her little girl
and that homicidal maniac brother
of hers plus all the red-headed
crazies from the neighborhood
circled the pool
like a school of piranhas.

There was a lot of dunking and cannonballs.
Parents sipped their piña coladas
in pagoda umbrella shade.

Barbie couldn't tell if the grownups
were hammered or just bored.

After the brother dumped
ice cubes down her bathing suit,
the little girl tucked Barbie into a fold
in her beach towel and ran screaming
into the house.

Around midnight Mother
shook out the rumpled towels.
Barbie felt herself fly through
cool night air. Without a whisper
she flipped into the water
and floated gently
on the surface of the pool.

Panic Attack

After she ran I heard the door slam.
She'll come back.
No she won't.
Where is she?
In this hot sun I could melt!
I'm suffocating here!
Where's her brother!
It's getting dark.
Am I dying?
No, I forgot, I can't die.
H E L P!

The First Night

My panic has subsided
a little. In the pool I feel
my polyvinyl chloride off-gassing.
Chlorine seeps into my
rooted synthetic fibers
with a tickling sensation.
My "ultra-soft" elastomer
seems to retain my elasticity.

I watch a bubble
from my interior cavity escape.
After that, gravity forces me
to the bottom of the pool.
On the way down I rock
back and forth like a pendulum.

The full moon ripples far above.
Those stars are not fixed.
In the pool, time speeds and drifts.
Like planets, an inflatable swan,
a bulbous shark
and a yellow and pink doughnut,
float above me.

Wrapped in space time,
I self-sooth.

The Day All I Could Think of Was Suburbia

I remember looking out the picture window
the sprinkler on the lawn twirled,
rainbows gleamed in fine mist,
robins tugged worms from the damp turf.
Compact SUVs filled with giggling cheerleaders
tooled past our split-level. Beyond the sidewalk
tree plumes sprouted at regular intervals.
There was a fire hydrant on every corner.

My little girl's mother clutched
her first drink of the morning
in her white-knuckled manicured hand.
She was a stay-at-home mom.
That day she wore her pink peignoir.

She scowled at me—
plucked me from the windowsill
and lifted my skirt.
I wasn't wearing undies.

I was born with eyes that can never close...

—Joy Harjo, Poet Laureate

Well not born exactly.
Can you imagine, me, Barbie, swimming
doing the scissor kick, swan dives,
the breast stroke—more my style—
synchronized into a Busby Berkeley
extravaganza. Get out your kaleidoscope.
I can perform this number all by myself
in stop-motion animation.

Peepers start Evensong in high C major.
I see a pink jet trail—puffy pink clouds.
Let me tell you about water, dark green
and purple underneath. Pink light retreats.
My mind drifts beneath a liquid blanket.
I hear your brother watching TV.
Mother is washing dinner dishes.
You are curled on your bed reading.

If the stars fell into this pool
would they hiss when they hit the water?
Would they sputter out and drown?
I lie here like a stunned mullet—
fishy and diluted—when cicadas
start their racket I might go out
of my mind. I miss sex. Then I imagine
Ken preening in front of his mirror.

My drowned eyes point toward the sky.

A Fall Day

The sky above melts
mellow as whiskey. Small
amber leaves flutter onto the pool.
Bubbles rise in sunrays' slow slant.
A rabble of crows swarms overhead,
the racket deafening. White
crow shit pierces the water's surface
like buckshot.

One day last fall my little girl's brother
dribbled his basketball on the patio.
Reverberations pinged and panged.
Suddenly he slammed the ball
hard against the clapboards.
Mother ran out the sliding door—
red-faced—suds dripping from her
caution-tape-yellow Playtex gloves.

I remember our sagging chain link fence,
The family's golden retriever dozed
in dappled light, three maples
writhed with colonies of stinkbugs.

Today maple seed pods helicopter
into the deep end of my pool
staining the water with tannin,
what a bitter taste.

I Feel So Small

Think mosquito larva
Think minnow
Think pencil lead
Think shot glass
Think flea
Think Chihuahua
Think bonsai
Think pinprick
Think Thumbelina
Think dust mote
Think cat penis
Think baby squid

Jesus can you see me
at the bottom of this pool?

The Weight of Loneliness

I would be lying
if I said I didn't miss you.
The way you mother me—
hold my small stiff hand.
You don't say, *shhh*
or, *it will be okay.*
My feelings drown me.
When we used to lie
beside each other,
and I felt your warm breath
pour over me,
we were inseparable,
stepping over puddles
and sidewalk cracks.
You would kiss me and tuck me bodily
in the crook of your neck.
I am sick from missing you,
as if I were swimming the length
of the Great Lakes. I know
if I hurtled over Niagara Falls,
you would be with me all the way
even without a barrel.

Barbie Gets Religion

An owl makes a noise
like a wishbone
is stuck in his throat.

I know this pool better than
the palm of my hand.
In between beach toys—
deflated as oil slicks on the surface—
a blanket of leaves obscures my view.
The drain clogged months ago.

I have been wet for so long,
I can't remember what it's like to be dry.
Dry is my new religion.
The Sun is my god.
The one thing I'm not is thirsty.

My idea of heaven is desert sand,
no oasis in sight—just rocks
and thorns and horny toads.
Zero percent humidity.

My heaven is a thick terry cloth towel.

Amphibian Dreams

About the frog—

I need to keep telling myself
he isn't human. But then
in the strictest sense,
neither am I.

I can't seem to forget him—
the way his abdomen
tapers to his crotch,
and his legs bend at the knee,
how, with a single powerful thrust
he shoots across the pool.

I fantasize his fishy grip,
his smooth belly snug up against me
his gold-flecked eyes peer into mine
and his tongue quivers
in his beaming mouth.

I feel elevated in my watery bed,
this drift. I reel and moan
in my uncalm inland sea.

Barbie Misses Her Little Girl

Dear Heart, she called me,
are you warm enough?
as she tucked me under a Kleenex.
She is my forever goddess—
my little girl almost forgotten.
Is she curled in sleep tonight?

She used to look me straight
in the eye, trying her best
to understand the world.

What was it like
when you were an astronaut?
A mother? A teacher? A chef?
A racecar driver? she'd ask.
I remember the small furrow
between her eyebrows
after each question.

When she gazes at her
softly twirling nightlight,
does she think of me?
Or does she feel abandoned?

Barbie Suffers from Insomnia

> *O Mother*
> *I love you*
> *despite*
> *everything.*
> —Erica Jong

To be deprived of sight and sound—
exhausted as a lobster in a trap—
unblinking—forced to a depth
where everything goes black.

Here my desires seem flimsy—
even water has lost its transparency.
Threads of bubbles syphon up
from my bed of leaf mold.

Dear Mother, are you on your
third Manhattan of the evening?
Is my little girl lost in fitful sleep?
Is your son under arrest yet?

You recite your Sylvia Plath—
wishing you could eat your X
like air. Is there viciousness
in your bathroom? Lie still—

pressed against the porcelain.
Keep your head above water—
holy and scummed with bath salts
while you float on the River Lethe.

Tell me what keeps you awake at night

suspended as in a dream.

Is it how overhead the maple's
weathered branches clutch at the web of stars,
meteors trail their sputtering tails,
and galaxies spin in blind darkness?

I recall reading Mother's *Cosmopolitan*—
it told us how to mesmerize a man.
I remember playing Pretty, Pretty Princess.
You held all your jewels close to your

baby breasts. Remember watching
the family black and white TV when Nixon
boarded Air Force One, his fingers
devil-horned into Vs for victory?

I feel part of me is missing. Think of me, Dear Girl.
I want to be quiet enough to hear you breathe.
I'm right here, steps away from where you are.
If I could hear you, I would sleep at night.

If only I could close my eyes.

Glass Half Full

That just about does it!
My bathing suit is gone
and here I am bare ass
at the bottom of the pool.

Not depressed maybe
but definitely submerged.
I keep telling myself—
at least I don't need to breathe.

I long for sleep.
In windless darkness
Northern lights glow
like ghost horsetails.

Water is my second skin
in my underwater half-life.
I'm no naiad. I wish I were dead—
either dead, or standing on dry land.

The Ice Has Begun to Unclench

The pool froze months ago. Above me,
bits of twigs and leaves suspend in a slab of gray.
My glass ceiling is an infinity mirror—a *mise en abyme*,
no more than a funhouse trick of misogyny,
cracked but unbroken—a barrier to a darker ceiling
of false sky. Looking up I see how fractals of stars limn
each leaf. I have no more choice than flotsam.
When this ice floe breaks up and melts will it make
any difference to me? Even my body isn't my own.

Title from a line by Ann Carson, "The Glass Essay"

Deep That Murmurs in My Shallows

I hear garbage cans rattle to the curb.
It's early. If I had tear ducts
I would cry. I think I might
be full of myself but it's only water
weighing me down.

Maybe my marriage was a figment
of my imagination. I don't see a ring.
The same question again and again
unanswered. Where are you Ken?
Are you lost too?

Variations on Drowning

As small as I am I could
drown in a mudpuddle.

I would like to see Ken
snoring beside me
in the bottom of this pool
as in a baptismal
and his soul in jeopardy.
I would watch him dream
while water passes
over and under
his toned body.

When he wakes
he could place his hand
in the small of my back
and help me
to the top of this
unfathomable water.

I would like to give him
a gnarled stick to lean on—
one that has a plum dangling
from a forked branch at the top.
I would like to blot this chlorine
from him with a beach towel.

I would like to be the air
touching him in a million places—
seeping into his lungs
with each breath.

How I wanted to be that sky—

—Ocean Vuong

I see now how light bends when it touches water.
Starlight needles to the bottom of my pool.
Satellites—silver ball bearings shoot in their arcs
transmitting either happy news or dire regrets.
My blank stare horizonless, my isolation tank full,
my heart swamped with remorse and hope—
every drop drowned in longing. At night
the pool's unfathomable weight hovers
between me and my desire, occasionally
interrupted by the Kleig light of the moon.

I Can't See the Top of the Pool

Dear Frog, Is it a coincidence—
the way our love is like
a single amoeba split in two?
You are my bioluminescence.
If only I could absorb you
like a sponge or a swallowed fishhook,
gobble your glisten from the bottom
of this upside-down world.
If this pool were upended I would be
on top. This could never happen, though.

I'm too sentimental. Today I thought
of my little girl, her pigtails flying,
sunlight glinting off her braces.
How she smiles when she catches
sight of me, the way we used to share
her peanut butter and banana sandwiches.
It gave me hope I hadn't felt in months.
Above me I see only a small rectangle
of the sky that surrounds
this mostly blue planet.
It's not that I don't still feel joy,
I do, but I will not forget this
overabundance of water.
I will never look at tears
the same way either, how they
course down dusty pink cheeks
and leave streaks like claw marks.

You are Not

my personal frog
as much as I want you to be—

nobody is that powerful.
You are merely my neighbor.

I should give up this absurdity
while you joyfully hop

from one lily pad to another.
Please permit me my humanity

as I permit you your animal nature.
I don't need your approval—

your signature on a form to make
our common-law marriage stick

instead of a technicality,
a misunderstanding,

a wound. I should submit
to an exorcism

with—or without—
your permission.

In This Country of Water

Barbie imagines she is a siren
drowning in the bottom of the pool.
What song should she sing to lure
the little girl's brother to dive in
and find her. She knows his breath
would be the last. Her song
should be heavy metal. Deep Purple
would be appropriate. If only
she had her boom box!
But her voice is so teensy
each bubble contains only one note.
Help! Barbie cries, *Help! Help! Help!*

The title is a line from Margaret Atwood's "Night Poem."

Water World Entire

Though I am not human,
I'm alive in my body,
a sleepless little mermaid
outside my shoebox
locked out of my motorhome
no chance of being a fire dancer
or a drunk. No one sees
my predicament.
Do they even wonder
what's become of me?
No one has come to my rescue.
In the sodden slipskin of my panic
I have this crazy impulse to go
home, regardless of how
impossible that is. Your safe
little room remains
in my mind, the quiet,
my bed, my fifty pairs
of stilettos. Under ten feet
of water I can't even turn over,
but at least I didn't settle face down.
In my mind I hear you calling.
As obsessed as I am, I want your hand
to pull me up. I want to hear
you say, I have you. Suddenly
you're carrying me—
swimming me right out
of this watery hell, both of us
happy and astounded.

The Dreadful Now

I'm thinking of chlorine
and a dream in which
tree frogs are singing.
I want to sleep with my heart
desiccated as a dried apricot,
but I am always falling
into the dreadful now.
I'm an adequate doll—
if not exactly a kind person.
I grieve appropriately.
I mourn this season
of extinctions as one
creature after another
tips under a crust of earth
or starves on a silver dollar
of melting ice.
I imagine a lone rhino
wandering hornless
across the Serengeti.
Yesterday a crow plunged
from the sky—spread eagle
onto the surface of my pool.
From where I am it looked
as if he were still flying—
except for his cold dead eye.
I wish I could take my little
girl to the mall and buy
a Ziploc bag of goldfish
to release into this pool.
How I would love
to watch them glimmer
and rise to the top to sip
small bubbles of air
delicious as gumdrops.
I'm thinking of the light
at dawn. I'm thinking
I'm heartbroken. I'm
thinking of catastrophe.

Sweetheart, I want to hold
onto you. More than
anything, I want you
to know where I am.

Feeling Soupish

—after Diane Seuss

My pool and I knit in a feral tangle—
water bugs skate across the tensile surface,
floating leaves support mating dragonflies.

Below spring sky—rain spatter
dilutes my gloomy tank. Branches
dormant until now untether new leaves.

If this is spring, I have endured
almost an entire revolution—
a wheel of seasons.

A mallard hen paddles across the pool's surface—
webs orange as sunrise—followed by eight ducklings.
I make out their rubber eraser feet.

Mother raccoon washes her haul
from the clanked over garbage can. Like tassels
her stripe-tailed babies suckle while she eats.

My frog must have found a mate. Frog eggs
green as grapes begin their gelatinous
wriggle. Soon I will be abandoned again.

Happiness eludes me.
If someone would throw coins into this pool
I could stack them and make my escape.

But this morning threads of sunlight, like hope,
twine among maple leaves, birds fledge,
and somewhere my girl is growing.

Perpetual Absence

Water became a gift Barbie felt
like a second skin, invisible, but
seen with her inner eye as a necessity—
protection from the external world.
There in her backwater, disregarded,
shaken off and ignored, scummy
water circulated—sluggish, and where
she was she couldn't be certain. She
wondered—for she was now entirely
within her head—if she were wrung dry
who would she be in her freedom?

Rescue

In the end my rescue isn't as dramatic
as I hoped it would be. No helicopter
chops through humidity above my pool.
No one drags the depths for my corpse.
Stirring music brings no tears
to onlookers eyes. There are no
onlookers. There is no music.
There is no kiss of life.
There is no kiss.

Worn steel-toed boots peek over
the lip of the pool. A vacuum hose
descends into the murk. I hear
labored breathing and a smoker's cough—
followed by ear-splitting sucking.
Bit-by-bit the surface of the water
comes closer. Too late I realize
I am addicted to water like crack.

Clouds flatten against the sky.
"Jerry"—the oval badge whipstitched
to his coveralls reads—is no
pool boy. His calloused hands rip
me from sodden leaves. I am born again.
Whole and naked into shattered daylight.
Transported and transfixed.
Limp as a drowned tulip.

I had forgotten the world—buzzing
power lines overhead, split concrete,
tar-oozing asphalt, cracks filled
with ants. Nervous, I am
as charged with electricity as an eel,
my future spread before me
like an empty pool.

Home
At Last

Needles Sharp as Regret

Remember when we went
on shopping trips with Mother,
you wrapped me in your pale blue
baby blanket cradled face forward
so that I could see where
we were headed.
I weighed next to nothing.
We looked for tiny buttons
at the five and dime.
You chose fabrics
with the tightest weave—
silk chiffon, scraps of velvet,
fur and selvages from Mother's
sewing projects, leftovers from
your own party dresses,
trims and hair ribbons
smelling of Prell shampoo
and Ivory soap sweet as you
after you soaked in your bath
and emerged tender as a cookie.
Your mother snipped cloth into shapes
for capes and pencil skirts. Tiny clothes
materialized under the whirring needle
of her Singer Featherweight,
stitches set at the smallest setting,
the needle going faster and faster—
every garment tinged
with the scent of nicotine.

Last Rites

I remember slumber parties
at your girlfriend's house
how in the dark room
headlights from passing cars
swept across the ceiling
and all the other Barbies
were flung down in disarray
after an orgy of undressing
and Ken kissing and you
were always the first one asleep.
One night the other girls
put their index fingers
beneath you and raised you
over their heads
like mourners carrying a casket
in a funeral procession.

Foreshadowing

She wants to be beautiful—
even more beautiful than Barbie.
She wants to wear all the makeup
on her mother's vanity, to sparkle
and glow in the dark so brightly
she won't cast a shadow.

She wants to run around naked—
her arms spread as wide as
the wings of a heron. She wants
to run wild, her lips glossed
and kissable, her hips electric
with titillation, in short shorts

or cut-offs rising up on her butt-
cheeks—her tits a total come-on.
She wants beautiful boys
to stumble when they see her
in her hot pink bikini. She wants
older girls to love her and hate her.

She wants to drain her mother's
Jim Beam and fill the bottle with
water. Bleach her hair platinum.
No more scabs on her knees.
No more braces. She thinks she's
immortal. She wants her first kiss.

Unobtainable

We are expected to be pretty and well dressed until we drop.
—Edith Wharton, "The House of Mirth"

Mother desired to be the best wife with the best life/thin hipped petal-lipped/stacked but skinny/perfumed and gullible/Stepford unobtainable/not easily maintainable/she stuffed her drawers with teddies and rhinestone zoris/wore makeup sultry and moody/dressed in ostrich mules and see-through tulles/pampered and manicured/ toenails polished/heels smoothed/ears pierced/ego soothed.

She piled her coffee table with magazines/romance novels and Dexatrim/stocked her bar with tequila/margaritas and mangos/ smoked oysters/Vienna sausages/green olives stuffed with pimento/ V-8 with vodka/cayenne/celery and a twist/she swilled/sucked and sucked-up Tab and Virginia Slims from morning until night/her expression an illusion/ a ring on her finger not in her tub.

The way she lived/some days she couldn't get off her hands and knees.

Today Barbie's in Love with Sex

I'm in love with a broke down
dollhouse. I'm in love with my girl
as tenuous as her love might be.
I'm in love with her smelly old sock
just because she wore it. What I mean is that
when we lost Ken at the bus station
sex was the last thing on my mind.
We didn't realize he was lost until
hours later. One time I fell in love with
a frog. He had just managed
to grow some feet. Then
he hopped away. I tried sex
with one of my shoes.
After that didn't work I quit trying.
I called my little girl's mother my mother
even though I knew she wasn't.
I tried to get a job at the Piggly Wiggly
but I couldn't reach the cash register.
Everyone treats me like an alien,
or a beauty queen. They hate me
for being white. They shame me
for forgetting what day it is,
and not remembering my multiplication
tables. They hate me for my perfection.

A woman in Odessa is my clone.
She calls me the golden mean.
Barbrification is the sincerest form
of flattery. Once a spider tried to bite me
but she couldn't puncture my plastic.
When I auditioned for my first movie
the director put his finger on my knee.
I ran away as fast as my little legs
would carry me. Ronan Farrow
gave me an interview. "Me too," I wailed.
I tried to get it on with a toy airman
just because he had flexible elbows and knees.
He was no Ken though. He only talked
about war and couldn't move his joints
without help. Today I'm in love with sex.
I can pleasure myself.

She Read to Me

I want to say something about
forgiveness, about how when I was new
the little girl and I were inseparable. When
she started school she read me every book
stacked in the orange crate beside her bed.
We read about frogs, toads, and a blue truck.
She pointed out pictures of all sorts of animals.
She read to me under the covers with a flashlight
while all the grownups were asleep.

And she really, really liked me.
I can't blame her for getting older.
Every year, she changed and changed.
She used to ask me if her breasts
would ever be as round and pointy
as mine. I couldn't find the right answer.
When her friends came over she tucked
me under her pillow. I waited up for her
to come home at night.

At first she painted her lips the same
sweetheart pink as mine, aqua powder
highlighted her eyes. Then
she had her ears pierced. Her lipstick
changed to black. She cut my hair
and stapled me to her backpack.
I was some kind of statement—or
an afterthought. When my head fell off
she didn't bother to pick it up. I don't
want to think about love anymore.

Barbie Tosses Her Head

Barbie flicks back her glossy synthetic waves.
It's easy, her arm bends stiffly at the elbow—
she sweeps her tresses in a slow arc
a flip of her head, her terrible beauty
as riveting as a majorette. If only
her teeth weren't always exposed—
saccharin—shark-like.

Her hair hasn't begun to lose its luster.
She has seen other Barbies, hair
matted and dull as a used scrub brush.
Hers still ripples like a silky waterfall.
Everyone notices.

Gravity means nothing to Barbie.
Her breasts are still firmly attached.
She has no nipples to get sore.
Neither does she have a uterus that will shrivel
and need to be removed. She will never wear
Depends. She knows she will always
be the golden girl.

But Barbie is lonely in her plastic box—
her closet filled with Versace dresses,
her little girl all grown up,
signing her third pre-nup,
undergoing the scalpel again,
eyebrows raised almost to her hairline.

I Feel I Understand Existence

—Vladimir Nabokov, "Pale Fire"

Although I may be no more than a tchotchke
on a shelf gathering dust that I will never return to—

my thoughts resurface as artifacts
lured to the present by something
I don't quite understand, succulent
as pieces of fruit in lime Jell-O
floating in my mind until relived
in multi-colored splendor.

I remember when my little girl's brother
wrapped me in a tinfoil shroud and buried
me in the garden like a time capsule. I was lucky
she saw him from her bedroom window.

I'm one of the juicy tidbits from her childhood
retrieved from her memory's playhouse.
She may suddenly recall other morsels
suspended beside me.

One month we thought Mother
was baking us Russian wedding cookies—
kitchen counters powdered with sugar
in drifts like snow. How old will my girl be
when she realizes that Mother was snorting
blow? That needle tracks up and down her arms
were not mosquito bites? When will my girl
admit her delinquent brother deserved
to be incarcerated?

That long ago day she pulled me
from deep earth—unwrapped me and smoothed
me over and over in her gentle hands
to make sure I was whole. I brushed away
the teardrop glistening on her cheek.
When will she remember where she's
concealed me? What box, what chest,
what burial?

Acknowledgments

"Writing Weird" was published by Mojave River Press, Fall/Winter 2018.

"Possession" is forthcoming in *The Poeming Pigeon: Pop Culture* (The Poetry Box, Fall, 2020).

"The Ice Has Begun to Unclench" and *"I was born with eyes that can never close..."* are forthcoming in *Willawaw Journal*, Winter 2020.

Addendum

"Barbie Suffers from Insomnia" was published
in *The Opiate*, November 2019.

"Unobtainable" and "I feel I understand Existance"
are forthcoming in *The Opiate* (Winter, 2020).

Notes

"*Running Water*"—after Suzy Harris,
"Late Summer Letter"

"*I Don't Want to Think About Love Anymore*"
—after Patrick Dundon,
"After He Said The End"

"*Taxonomy of Lost Things*"
—Title a quote from Bruce Smith in a review
describing the work of Paul Guest.

I need to make it clear that this collection is not a "selfie" by any stretch of the imagination.

My children have been marvelously supportive every step of the way. My son Jesse and his wife Marjorie have heard me read some of these poems over the din of motorcycles and leaf blowers, coffee grinders and fire sirens. My daughter Lisa has been patient through many shaky first readings and when my youngest son Andrew Skypes from Europe invariably our conversation will end with a "Barbie." None of them has been in foster care.

My mother is my biggest fan! We spend hours each week discussing the relative merit of one word or another. I have never seen her touch a drop.

I have dragged my husband to poetry readings too numerous to mention and yet he wrote me the wonderful foreword to this collection although he didn't want me to say so.

I don't have a brother.

Until last week I hadn't owned a Barbie.

My gratitude to all those who've gone on this crazy trajectory with me, *Thank You!* Oregon poets you know who you are.

Colette Tennant made many refinements to *The Barbie Diaries* manuscript. Her brilliant editing taught me skills I will use going forward.

Sherri Levine and I have been fellow poets since we read two years ago. Together we kept the audience laughing. Sherri was instrumental in getting this book off the ground.

Poet and editor, Rachel Barton has encouraged my writing by publishing several of my poems plus two of my "Barbies" in her wonderful *Willawaw Journal*.

Poet, teacher, inspiration, and "bad influence" Penelope Scambly Schott likes my sense of humor.

Artist and cousin Peggy Manring has been my best friend since we were toddlers. We loved our Cottage Dolls as much as most girls loved their Barbies.

Poet Carolyn Adams asked me to "write weird" and this book is the result.

DALE CHAMPLIN is a new poet living in Hillsboro, a small town in Western Oregon. Her MFA is in fine arts, not poetry. She is the editor the *Verseweavers* poetry anthologies of winning poems from Oregon Poetry Association contests, and director of Conversations With Writers, a monthly presentation by accomplished writers leading spirited discussions about the craft of writing. Dale has published in *VoiceCatcher, North Coast Squid, Willawaw Journal, Mojave River Press, The Voices Project* and other publications. During the month of January, 2019 Dale wrote a poem a day as part of the Tupelo Press 30/30 Project.

Made in the USA
Lexington, KY
20 November 2019